BARBARA G. MARTHAL

Illustrated by:
AVERY LIELL-KOK

# FIGHTING FOR FREEDOM

## ——— A DOCUMENTED STORY ———

AuthorHouse™
1663 Liberty Drive
Bloomington, IN 47403
www.authorhouse.com
Phone: 833-262-8899

Because of the dynamic nature of the Internet, any web addresses or links contained in this book may have changed
since publication and may no longer be valid. The views expressed in this work are solely those of the author and do not
necessarily reflect the views of the publisher, and the publisher hereby disclaims any responsibility for them.

Any people depicted in stock imagery provided by Getty Images are models,
and such images are being used for illustrative purposes only.
Certain stock imagery © Getty Images.

This book is printed on acid-free paper.

ISBN: 978-1-4772-2922-4 (sc)
ISBN: 978-1-4772-6133-0 (e)

Library of Congress Control Number: 2012911861

Print information available on the last page.

Published by AuthorHouse  02/22/2021

authorHOUSE®

# FIGHTING FOR FREEDOM
## —— A Documented Story ——

by
**Barbara G. Marthal**

**Dedicated to my grandchildren, Jasmine and NaDavion
With special thanks to my husband, Bill Harris, SCV**

## Author's Note

In **Fighting for Freedom**, the author uses primary source documents to re-construct the story of a young Confederate soldier and his servant who join the Tennessee militia in 1861 and become a part of the Tennessee Brigade, Army of Northern Virginia. The story tells why they fought, how the servant gets his freedom and what happens to them after the war. The purpose of the book is to help children understand how research skills can be put to use to tell the stories of our ancestors. The servant in this story married the author's first cousin three times removed.

# FIGHTING FOR FREEDOM

"There are just too many fire eaters in Tennessee! That's what pa said he heard your daddy say the other day. Are there people who eat fire," Handy asked Richard as they sat fishing one mild Saturday afternoon in 1861.

Richard laughed, "No Handy. Once I saw a man at the fair that made it look like he ate fire, unsettling yes but not real. The fire eaters my father spoke of are the people who want the southern states to secede from the Union as a stand for "states' rights." More southerners are supporting secession but they are a minority in Tennessee. Tennesseans voted against a state convention on secession in February."

Richard, the son of Isham F. and Sarah Bradshaw Davis was born in April, 1843 on a large farm in the Silver Springs community of Wilson County, Tennessee. He had a dark complexion, dark hair, hazel eyes, and was 5 feet 10 inches tall. Richard's father owned three slave families one of which was the family of Handy Davis Crudup, born in 1846, to Nancy Davis Crudup.

Handy had a rich brown complexion and stature similar to Richard's. They were close companions. Born on the same farm, they had spent many days working, hunting, fishing and playing together since early childhood.

They listened closely to talk in the community which was becoming more heated everyday. What Richard had dismissed on the creek bank about Tennessee having few fire eaters had changed entirely by May.

Why did Tennesseans become fire eaters? Two big events helped them make the change; (1) the Battle of Fort Sumter, April 12, 1861 and (2) President Abraham Lincoln's call for 75,000 soldiers to invade the south. In other words, Mr. Lincoln "ruffled our feathers."

This was our response:
> *Resolved by the General Assembly of the State of Tennessee,* That the
> refusal of the Governor of this State to furnish troops in compliance with
> the call of Abraham Lincoln, meets the cordial approval of this body, and
> reflects the will of the State.
> *Resolved further,* That the people of Tennessee will resist with all their
> power and to the last extremity, any attempt on the part of the Govern-
> ment at Washington to invade or subjugate the Southern states.
> W. C. Whitthorne,
> Speaker of the House of Representatives.
> B. L. Stovall
> Speaker of the Senate
> Adopted April 27, 1861

On May 6, the State Legislature adopted the Ordinance of Secession which was affirmed by popular vote on June 8.

Richard was zealous for duty to Tennessee and the Confederate States of America. He talked of enlisting in the Tennessee militia. Handy had no intentions of being left behind. No one was surprised by their decision. Just about every family in Sliver Springs and the surrounding communities had sons who readily joined them.

With a gathering of family and friends to cheer them on, they left for Nashville early Monday morning, May 20. Richard eagerly enlisted accompanied by an equally confident Handy. Like everyone else, they felt the matter of teaching the Yankees a lesson would not take long, so Richard signed up for a year.

Selected files from Richard's Military Records

7

Nashville, Tennessee Railroad Depot

Richard and Handy were assigned to the 7th Tennessee Infantry Regiment, Company I, "The Silver Spring Guards," with Captain Joseph A. Anthony, under the command of Colonel Robert Hopkins Hatton. The brigade was mustered into Confederate service in July, entrained and reached Staunton, Virginia on July 25, 1861. There, with other Tennessee Infantry Regiments, they formed the Tennessee Brigade, Army of Northern Virginia, under Brigadier General Samuel R. Anderson.

General Joseph E. Johnston                    Major General Thomas J. Jackson.

Winchester, Virginia was very important to the Confederate States Army. General Joseph E. Johnston and Major General Thomas J. Jackson set up the defense of the Shenandoah Valley. The Tennessee brigade and the Danville Artillery, commanded by Captain Lindsay M. Shumaker joined General Jackson at Winchester in December 1861. On January 4, 1862, Richard and Handy were among the men of the brigade that went with General Jackson to Bath, Virginia to destroy the railroad bridge.

On May 23, 1862 Colonel Hatton was promoted to Brigadier General and given command of the Tennessee brigade. Richard and Handy fought with the brigade at the Battle of Seven Pines when General Hatton was killed on the 31st of May. Richard was severely wounded in the knee which left him permanently disabled for field service. Handy went to his aid on the battlefield. Richard was sent to Richmond for recuperation. Handy accompanied him and helped nurse him back to health.

After a furlough, both were determined to return to duty. Richard was reenlisted by Captain William. E. Curd and Handy joined him. Richard was assigned to the Quarter Master Department in Richmond, April 1863. In February 1864, having fulfilled his assignment in Richmond, Richard wrote a letter requesting a transfer and service under General J. E. Johnston of the Army of Tennessee in Oconee, Georgia. Richard and Handy were in Oconee by March 1st.

Office of Q.M.Dept.
Richmond Va
Febry 10th 1864

Sir:

I have the honor to Submit herewith an application for a transfer to the portions of the army under the command of Gen'l J. E. Johnson (Army of Tennessee) to be allowed to report for duty to Capt I. G. McKee Inspector of field transportation at Oconee Georgia. I submit the following as the basis of my application.

I am a member of Co. I. 7th Tenn. Reg't. permanently disabled. from the effects of a gun shot wound in the knee, received at the Battle of Seven Pins. Since my partial recovery from the effects of Said wound I have been detailed by the Secretary of War and on duty as agent in charge of army baggage, at first acting under orders from Maj. C. D. Hill and recently from those of Maj. Bently. As appears from the enclosed recommendation of Capt. Cone. Act. Asst. Q. M. Gen'l there are no further need for my services in that capacity. I have the honor to Submit a request from Capt. McKee that I should be transferred to that department, and be permitted to report to him for duty at Oconee Georgia. This I am very anxious to have done one of which is that I think I can render my country more efficient Service there than here.

Hoping this request will meet your approval,
I have the honor to remain,
Very Respectfuly
Your obt Svrt

S. Cooper, A. & I. G.          R. T. Davis
Present,                        sni. Co. I. 7th Tenn.

Richard's request for transfer

Selected files from Richard's Military Records

REBEL NEGRO PICKETS AS SEEN THROUGH A FIELD GLASS,

Harper's Weekly, January 10, 1863.

Handy was one of tens of thousands of people of African descent that served and worked in the Confederate Army. Few of them were officially enlisted as soldiers but they were there none the less. They fought and served with no less commitment than those of enlisted men. Most were "slaves" but some were "free people of color." Historical papers, military records, pension files and testimonies, tell of the brave and vital contributions they made to the Confederate States Army. They repaired railroads, built fortifications, worked as teamsters, cooks, blacksmiths, musicians, drummers, nurses, color bearers, spies, pickets, body guards, sharp shooters and much more. Women of African descent also served the Confederacy and a few of them also received pensions.

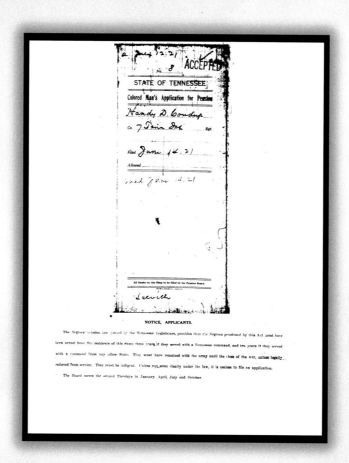

Selected files from Handy Davis Crudup's Pension Application

**General Robert E. Lee**

In 1864 General Lee said, "When you eliminate the black Confederate soldier, you've eliminated the history of the South."

**General Nathan Bedford Forrest**

General Forrest took with him from his plantation 42 men of African descent. He asked them to drive his ambulances and wagons. He told them that if the North won, they would be free and if the South won he would set them free. Eighteen months before the war ended he gave them their free papers for fear that he might be killed before the war's end. In late August 1868, General Forrest gave an interview to a reporter. Forrest said of the black men who served with him: "...these boys stayed with me...and better Confederates did not live."

During the last months of the war, Handy and Richard were assigned to a detail that rendered support to General Nathan Bedford Forrest. While Richard served in the Quarter Master Department, Handy was assigned to field support. Handy surrendered with his unit in April 1865. Richard surrendered at Guntersville, Alabama, May 20, 1865 and took the Oath of Allegiance in Nashville, June 21st.

Banners of the Confederacy

Although a slave, Handy lived his life with a personal sense of freedom and determination. He defended that sense of self when he joined his young master and friend to protect the rights of the state of Tennessee. He was given his legal freedom on February 22, 1865 when the people of the state agreed to a referendum to abolish slavery in Tennessee.

You may have thought Abraham Lincoln's Emancipation Proclamation freed Tennessee slaves but it did not. Mr. Lincoln exempted Tennessee from following his proclamation because parts of Tennessee were occupied by the Union army. He also exempted the slave states of Kentucky, Maryland, Delaware, New Jersey and Missouri.Handy was freed by the people of the state of Tennessee, a right for which he and Richard had gallantly fought. The sacrifices made on southern soil guaranteed immediate and future freedom.

Senior Preparatory Class,
Fisk University, Nashville, Tennessee

Model School, Fisk University,
Nashville, Tennessee

Roger Williams University-
Nashville, Tennessee-Normal Class

**Monroe Gooch,**
(cook) Confederate Army of Middle
Tennessee Infantry

**Andrew M. Chandler and Silas Chandler,**
Company F, 44th Regiment Mississippi Infantry.

Unidentified Portrait,
African American Woman

Warren C. Coleman, African American
Founder of Coleman Manufacturing Company
Concord, NC

Young Unidentified
African American Woman

After the war Richard and Handy returned to the Davis family farm. Handy married Louisa McFarland and Richard married Rachel J. Winter. Two new families shared the personal pride and joy of these brave young men. They worked the Davis farm together until Handy began farming for himself and working on the railroad. As neighbors and friends, each provided for their family and community.

Marlboro Camp
40th Georgia Infantry
Army of Tennessee

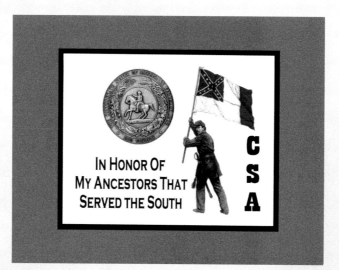

General Stand Watie
Cherokee Leader
Last Confederate General
to surrender

Members of the 57th Georgia Regiment
Army of Tennessee, 1863. Left to right,
First Lieutenant Archibald C. McKinley,
Captain John Richard Bonner, Scott (cook),
and Second Lieutenant William S. Stetson

Confederados: Many of the troops and officers
of the Confederate Army were of Mexican and
Spanish descent, including these officers of the
3rd Texas Calvary, CSA. They are left to right:
Reugio Benavides, Atanacio Vidurri,
Cristobal Benavides, and John Z. Leyendecker

18

General Robert H. Hatton Monument, Lebanon, Tennessee

Richard T. Davis is buried at Cedar Grove Cemetery in Lebanon, Tennessee as is General Robert H. Hatton. A stature of General Hatton stands in the town square of Lebanon. Handy Davis Crudup is buried in an unmarked grave near Mount Juliet, Tennessee. **They like many others have passed on but are not forgotten because we remember their valor.**

# Ode to Ancestors Who Were Slaves
## by Barbara G. Marthal

Early in the making of America
Our ancestors were there
They were the slaves
They turned the soil, planted the rice, the cotton, the corn, the
Tobacco and indigo,
They were the guides, the cooks, the butchers, and the bakers

Early in the making of America
Our ancestors were there
They were the slaves
They cleared the forests, produced the pitch, harvested the maple
They were the carpenters, the brick masons, the blacksmiths, the groomsmen and cattlemen,

Early in the making of America
Our ancestors were there
They were the slaves
They shared in the arms of early defense
They shared the arms of independence
They were the fighters, the nurse, the spy, and the music makers

Early in the making of America
Our ancestors were there
They were the slaves
They tended births and they tended deaths
They were midwives, comforters, the greeters of new life, and they bid the dead farewell

Early in the making of America
Our ancestors were there
They were the slaves
Their blood soaked into the American soil and runs deep within the veins of many of America's people
They were doctors, teachers, lawyers, statesmen, merchants, and grand ladies

Early in the making of America
Our ancestors were there
They were the slaves
They were the beloved and the mistreated
They were mothers, fathers, sisters, brothers, cousins, uncles, aunts, grandmothers, and
grandfathers of many

Early in the making of America
Our ancestors were there
They were the slaves
Thus I stand here before you this day
A proud descendant of slaves
Because early in the making of America
Our ancestors were there
They were the slaves

# A Slave's Vision
## by Barbara  G. Marthal

Standing in this past
Looking out into this present
Many speak of what was done to me
Few remember what I did for myself

Many speak of my bondage
Few know how I harnessed freedom

Sometimes I ran
Sometimes I purchased freedom
Sometimes I waited on the Lord
Sometimes freedom was through birth
Sometimes through violent rebellion
Sometimes freedom was in spirit amidst chains
But always my work was for freedom

Many know of my sorrows
Few know the happiness of my indomitable Spirit
That I loved and lost and loved again
Told stories to my children and my charges
Danced many nights to the sound of ancient rhythms
Soothed many a frighten soul with the hum of a melodic voice

Many speak with rage of my mistreatment
Few speak of my contributions and triumphs
The sweat of my brow, the strength of my back, the drops of my blood, the quickness of my wit, the hue
of my skin
Reminded others that the ideal of "freedom, justice, and equality" requires constant vigilance and work.

# GLOSSARY

**company** – a part of an army commanded by a captain, usually 100 men

**CSA**– Confederate States Army

**CSA** – Confederate States of America – the official eleven southern states that withdrew form the United States of America to form an independent country; South Carolina, Mississippi, Florida, Alabama, Georgia, Louisiana, Texas, Virginia, Arkansas, Tennessee, North Carolina. Some people considered Kentucky and Missouri as part of the Confederacy but they were never officially admitted.

**entrained** – to put on a train, to get on a train

**epilogue** – the concluding section sometimes added and serving to round out or interpret the work

**exempted** – did not require

**fire eater** – a person who supported the withdrawal of southern states from the United States of America for the purpose of forming a separate and independent country

**free people of color** – before to the Civil War, people of African descent who were no longer slaves or had never been slaves. More of them lived in the South prior to the Civil War than anywhere else in the United States of America.

**furlough** – time off from duty for military people

**infantry** – soldiers trained, equipped, and organized to fight on foot

**muster** – assemble for service

**occupied** – captured and controlled

**quarter master** – (in the army) an officer who has charge of providing quarters (place to live or stay), clothing, fuel, transportation, etc. for troops

**regiment** – a unit of troops made up of two or more battalions

**ruffled** – to cause a rise in anger

**secede** – to withdraw from a group or an organization as the thirteen colonies did from England to form the United States of America or as the Southern states did from the United States of America to form the Confederate States of America

**teamster** – during the civil war, anyone who drives a team of horses or mules

**zealous** – filled with passion and enthusiasm

# POINTS OF DISCUSSION

1. Select one individual, event or location from this book for research so that you can share more information on the life and times of Richard and Handy.

2. Visit your local or state library and cemetery to find civil war soldiers that may be buried and fought near you.

3. Do you have ancestors who fought in the civil war? If so share what you know about them.

4. Every infantry regiment marched to a drum or rhythmic song; do some research and share some of the music to which Handy and Richard may have marched.

5. Use the link given below to the Colored Confederate Pension Application Index to find another rebel of African descent who served the CSA.

6. Many young men who were the same age of Richard and Handy had not traveled far from home. Prepare a map that shows the locations and some of the distances they traveled during the war.

7. Tell of a time when you and a friend set out on a grand adventure.

8. The Confederate States of America had three national flags called the First National, the Second National and the Third National, and a well known battle flag. Put your research and artistic skills to work; prepare drawings or pictures and information about each flag. You may also include other flags of the Confederacy not mentioned here.

# BIBLIOGRAPHY

American Memory Library of Congress.  Library of Congress, Prints and Photographs Division.  Washington, D. C.

Ancestry.com  http://www.ancestry.com

Barrow, Charles Kelly, J. H. Segars, and R. B. Rosenburg, ed. Black Confederates. Pelican Publishing Company, 2004.

Colored Confederate Pension Application Index, Tennessee Archives.  http://www.tn.gov/tsla/history/collections/ccpa/index.htm

Fold3. http://www.fold3.com

Georgia College, 231 W. Hancock St., Milledgeville, GA 31061

Great War of the Confederacy, Kings Mountain, NC 28086.  http://www.rebelstore.com

Segars, J. H. and Charles Kelly Barrow, ed. Black Southerners in Confederate Armies: A Collection of Historical Accounts. Pelican Publishing Company, 2007.

Tennesseans in the Civil War Web Page http://www.tngenweb.org/civilwar/csainf/csa7.thml

Tennessee State Library and Archives, 403 7th Avenue North, Nashville, Tennessee.

Printed in the United States
By Bookmasters